Will You Ever Meet Me Again.

Dr Om Prakash Yadava

Dr Om Prakash Yadava

ISBN13:978-1515046387
ISBN-10:1515046389

PAPER COVER PRICE:$8

DEDICATION

Author is indebted to all those who have made sacrifices for upliftment of down trodden people of India and in return have got only sufferings & sufferings and also their services have gone unrecognized by the official set up of the governments.

CONTENTS

PROLOGUE.

Evening was fast approaching ,the blazing sun was bidding good bye to the land and dusk was getting ready to envelope the whole surroundings just waiting to see the last sun ray to disappear behind the hillock of dunes. He had still to travel a distance of over two kilometers on a dust laden pathway where he was all alone.he looked to his right,he looked to his left, he looked ahead as far as he could see,he turned back &looked behind but no body else was visible on the pathway or around the pathway.The feeling of being solitary on an unknown path was creating a sense of tremor in him and he was moving as fast as he could do,to reach the village before the darkness pervaded,where he was to stay and open a new chapter of his life.He had already travelled for over eighteen hours in the train to reach the railway station nearest to the place.That was a horrible journey full of shocking & unforgettable experiences though traveling in a reserved sleeper class but he had found all sorts of nuisance going on amongst the passengers and also train was halting very frequently even on unscheduled halts.During night hours some robbers had attacked the train and his compartment had also become a victim of their robbery.They had beaten some passengers and two women passengers had been robbed of their ornaments and belongings.Fortunately except some clothing and daily use items kept in a bag,he had nothing with him and the robbers had left that untouched.Having the taste and nightmare of wonderful train journey he had reached the last station of his journey around nine hours in the morning and alighted at the platform.He had no knowledge of the place and also how to proceed further and only a faint idea had been given to him that he had to take a bus and reach another stop where from he will have to move a distance of around five kilometers on foot to reach his final destination.

He enquired some gentleman about the waiting room who told him that station being small one just had a small place which could be considered as waiting room though lavatory facilities were available there.He came to that waiting room and had his morning routine and a wash of himself in the lavatory which was not properly maintained but he had no other option.He took some tiffin in a nearby small food stall and asked the counter boy about the bus station who directed him to go westwards on the road outside the station for about half a kilometer and therefrom he could get the bus for his destination.The journey in a government roadways transport bus was nerve breaking but since he had decided to keep himself above the world of pleasure & pain,humiliation & harassment,agony& grief and that was giving him strength to face every odd and yet advance towards his target place.Road journey had taken him three hours to reach the stop where he concluded his journey though that place was hardly sixty kilometers away from the railway station.The real test of journey was from there up to the village where he was destined to reach ultimately.

Oh my God ! he took a sigh and thought anxiously what all was waiting for him in the store ever since he had joined the mission of serving the suffering humanity through the Charity organization only a few months back that suddenly his eyes fell on the waning sun who was just on the brink of hiding behind the hillock.Oh ! such a bewitching beauty,such a radiance,such an aura as if a gold sheet heated to redness had been spread all over the entire sky before his eyes.He got himself lost in the miraculous yet enchanting splendor of nature and the thought which spontaneously came to his mind,

"whether some one treats sun as a god or as a celestial body or as a planet or as a star or as the head of our solar system,whatsoever,may be some one's perception but without bothering for that sun is endlessly giving to the earth,the light,the heat,the radiance, the brightness and of course elixir of life to all living creatures small & big irrespective of the fact whether some one worships him, recognizes him or treats him just as a

natural phenomenon.No body knows when and how sun came into being and how long he will continue to shine.everything is continuously undergoing change but sun is remaining unchanged and unfettered giving the same light and the same life to the world expecting nothing in return from any one.Really wonderful,possibly sun is not only defining but living the life of selfless karma (Nishkam Karma) as defined by Lord Krishna in Bhagvat Geeta."

While engrossed in his deep thoughts he could not notice that he had moved quite a long distance and the darkness had enveloped the whole environment pushing behind the dusk that   suddenly he saw some small lights of the burning lamps which were probably coming from the houses of the village.His attention got diverted and he realized that he had approached the village where he had to finally land.That gave him a sense of satisfaction but also an anxiety regarding his life ahead in an unknown place located in such an isolated area,however,he had left himself to his fate and in the hands of Almighty.

As he entered the village area he saw some youth sitting on a small dilapidated culvert and chit chatting something.He asked them about the school of the village where he was to meet another volunteer of his organization.

" You look to be an stranger,what makes you come to our village," enquired one of the young men.
" Yes ,I am not from this area,I am coming here for the first time.I am a volunteer of the charity organization and like to join my other colleague who is already rendering his services to your area," replied he.

The young men stood up with respect and one of them offered to escort him to the school premises where he would get his colleague. He thankfully acknowledged the help and marched along with the young man.The other volunteer Ranjan was eagerly waiting for him and greeted him as soon as he reached there.He thanked the young man and expressed his hope to have beautiful time ahead with them.

It was a village school housed in an old structure where boys and girls both were getting education up to tenth standard and in one corner of that structure a room had been earmarked for the people of that charity organization. Ranjan was staying there and thereafter the new colleague Sanatan would also stay with him.Room had some leaf mats,a pair of pillows,a few cooking utensils and clothing of Ranjan,an almirah and few pegs mounted on the walls for hanging the clothes and a lantern which was burning at that point of time,a kerosene stove and some cans and a few small small items as the total property and assets.There was a small battery of toilets located on the backside of the school which was being used by volunteers,teachers and also by the students of the school.

Ranjan lit the old stove kept in a corner of the room,put water in a small pan over it,added some sugar,milk & tea leaves and prepared tea and offered the same to Sanatan along with some eatables. Sanatan took a vessel of water,came out of the room,washed his hands,feet and face,wiped the face with a towel taken out of his bag and then sat on a mat spread on the floor and took the tea along with Ranjan.

" How was your journey and how do you feel now," asked Ranjan.

" I had a very long and arduous journey.In fact earlier to this I never had experience of traveling in a sleeper class of the Indian Railways.I had a glimpse of some reality of life.I had a variety of experiences during my train journey and subsequently during bus journey also.I also travelled such a long distance on foot for the first time.But any way I have mentally prepared myself to face truth and realities ahead and face whatever comes on the way but I will remain committed to my mission and try to do whatever good would be possible at my hands," replied Sanatan.

" Oh! good,that is the spirit behind us and that is our mission that makes me also to

be here in totally unfamiliar and unknown place practically living a deserted but dedicated life hoping nothing beyond improving upon the lives of people in these villages which are yet to see the light of the day.Any way now you relax.I will prepare some food for both of us and to-morrow morning I will explain to you of the life which you might have to have ahead."

Ranjan lit his stove again and prepared a simple food consisting of a mix of rice and pulse in a small time span of fifteen minutes and asked Sanatan to get up who was by then half asleep.He got up and both of them took the meals together in metallic plates. After the meals were over they washed their hands and mouth using the water kept in a pitcher and also washed the plates and cooking utensil. Ranjan spread another leaf mat on the floor and both of them lied down side by side. Sanatan was already feeling tired of the long and tiresome journey and he immediately went into deep slumber despite the fact that he was going to sleep on a mat spread on the hard ground for the first time in his life till then.

It was bright sun shining on the eastern horizon the rays of which had entered the room through the window that made Sanatan wake up.he got up,sat down on the mat rubbing his eyes with his hands to assure himself that it was the bright sun quite high in the sky. He was amazed to find that it was quite late in the morning and Ranjan had already completed his morning routine and was ready for the day having prepared the breakfast.he felt ashamed to himself as he was early morning riser and very punctual in his routine & habits but it was the mental & physical tiredness of the journey which had made him sleep so long on a hard uncomfortable bed. Ranjan gave him a cup of tea which he readily gulped in and thereafter Ranjan explained him all that he had to do to get himself freshened up and be ready.

" Let us take our breakfast quickly and thereafter I will take you around this village

and get you introduced to some old and prominent people of the village who will be of help to you and show all other houses."

Sanatan was still not out of the trauma of his journey and the tiredness which had affected his entire body and mind but he remembered that a soldier in the battlefield facing the raging enemy guns had no time to think of himself and his family left behind somewhere but to fight with all his might,skill and courage to protect himself & win and he immediately got up and went to the toilet and bath rooms side with tooth brush,paste,soap and towel in his hands.

Within half an hour he was back in the room having finished his morning routine.He dressed himself properly and combed his hairs,wore his shoes and got ready. Ranjan and Sanatan both took their breakfast just standing holding plates in their hands during which time Ranjan gave him a brief of the village,it's problems which he had encountered and the things that he could do.He also explained Sanatan to concentrate on that village for some days and once he became fully familiar then he could expand his activities to other areas and during that period he would take care of other villages.

They finished their breakfast,came out of the room,closed the door and locked it and taking with them shoulder hung cloth bags containing a diary,some biscuits and water bottles set out on foot to have a round of the village which though not very big but was quite scattered.

Ranjan took him one by one to every house,introduced Sanatan to elders and other known family members of the house.Every house,they were offered something to eat and something to drink.Somewhere,they took them and at some places they thankfully declined them.During this exercise Sanatan was very keenly observing the behavior of people,their response towards them,the common problems of the village and the philosophy of their life.They did not feel like taking some food for lunch but when it was very hot during mid day they preferred to relax for a couple of hours below a shady tree. In fact Sanatan found such trees to be only a few.While relaxing they took biscuits and water which they were carrying with them in their bag.afternoon Ranjan took him to other remaining houses of the village and completing the first day's task Sanatan came back to the room by the evening.The sojourn was over and the preamble of a new chapter of his life had been engraved on the stone walls of the time.

CHAPTER .I- The Departure.

"How! will I forget you ? You are an oasis,a palm tree in the desert of my heart,a glass of cold water for a traveller in hot sun,a peaceful evening with a cool breeze in the perched dry land of my psyche,a tranquilizer of my inner self,a dream of my being and over and above everything else which I can think of,you are my life.In fact I had forgotten myself,my life,my being on the earth but you have given me a burning flame to live a life.No,no I will never forget you,wherever,I may be,I will always be with you but what about you ? Will you always remember me?said Sanatan.

"I will wait for you till the last day of my life on this Mother Earth.Either I will unite with you to have a happy conjugal life or I will remain as such but definitely I will never have a family life if I don't get you,"replied Roshani.

"This is a very difficult promise you are making,will it really be possible to do that if something unexpected happens to me?"

" Why not.You know I belong to a breed,a creed where sacrifices are the way of life

and promises are always kept & never broken."

" You know,I am going to a place where risk and hazards are at every step and God! forbid,if some thing undesirable happens to me,then what will you do."

" First thing,I don't think on that line and in case the most unfortunate happens,I will accept that as my fate and succumb to my destiny but still I will not desist away from my determination.If I think of a bondage that would be only with you otherwise I will continue the way I am and what else to do next will be decided depending on the circumstances."

"My God !you are such a powerful woman,I never even dreamt of.Ok, I fully honor your words,your emotions and of course your decision & determination and I assure you that I will stand with you and for you ever."

"So,when are you leaving for your new destination?"

"To-morrow morning.Should I feel this is my last meeting with you ?"

" No,no.This is beginning of our meetings of unity.I may consider that after this meeting between us, you are going on *some other assignment which I want you to complete within a couple of years and thereafter let us start a new chapter of joint life."*

" Ok,ok.Agreed.Now be happy."

They could not speak much further,however,continued sobbing and weeping sitting very close to each other.Though Sanatan had been assuring and reassuring Roshani that he was going there just for a couple of years to complete a mission which was always his cherished desire after which he would leave the missionary work and settle down at his native place along with her.But she was not convinced and that some apprehension was looming large around her mind.She had tried her best to persuade him to desist away from going to his new place and continue there itself and after sometimes marry her and march towards future life,but Sanatan was very keen to go on his new assignment of charity.In this conflict of thoughts between the two which was there for several days,at length time had reached for him to depart leaving behind her in the darkness of his absence but in the light of his remembrances.

She remembered of the legendary last night when adolescent Lord Krishna was leaving Gokul for going to Mathura-the kingdom of demon king Kansa.It was the dead of night that Lord Krishna after having taken leave from every animate and inanimate being was sitting below a Kadamb tree and waiting for Radha to come and meet him so that he could take leave of her.Radha came,she was deep in tears.She sat by his side,tears rolling down her eyes.Lord Krishna stretched his right leg,she lied down putting her head on his leg.Her tear drops started falling on his ankle and sole.Both continued weeping for each other for a long time till it became mid night.Ultimately they bade good bye to each other,Krishna consoling her with the advice that wherever and whenever she thought of Him,He would be there in front of her eyes.Though after His departure Radha used to see Him everywhere in everything even in small creatures,flower petals and leaves but she could never meet Him again.After many years Krishna was hit by a hunter's arrow at the same place of His leg where tear drops of Radha had fallen on that fateful night and that resulted into His death.

Roshani got badly disturbed with the chain of her thoughts that if a similar story repeated to her,she would never be able to meet Sanatan again and possibly her rest of life may become aimless.Sobbing & weeping in those thoughts when did she reach back her home,she could not know that her father called her for his medicines.She gave medicines to her father and gave him a glass of warm water for taking them.He lied down on the cot and she went inside in the kitchen to help her mother who was preparing for cooking the dinner.She was doing everything in a manner that she could look normal and her parents might not be able to notice any iota of disturbance raging her mind.She was helping her mother but the way her hands were moving mother was able to guess that something was disturbing her .

"I have never seen you working erratic like this.Is there something going on in your mind,"asked Roshani's mother.

"No,no,nothing.I am normal,"replied Roshani but she herself was amazed that her voice was tumbling & trembling.

"See,I am your mother,you can't hide yourself from me.I find your body is telling something and your tongue is telling something else.Tell me very frankly what is disturbing you?"-

"No,no,nothing,just I have a little headache."

"You don't even know,how to speak a lie.Things are written on your face and body both that something very serious is disturbing you.Better tell me.I may share your worry and problem."

"Mummy ! you know Sanatan is going away to-morrow and I have a number of apprehensions in my mind.I don't know,why so many bad thoughts are coming to me and some premonition is continuously haunting me.No doubt,I know he is a man of very strong character and whatever,he says he does that and he has assured me to come back to me but I am

not getting convinced and these thoughts are disturbing me."

"Why don't you try then to stop him from going away."

"I have done my best but he is determined to go away.Though he says that he would be there just for two years and after that he will leave the missionary work and settle down as a family man with me in his native place but despite all that something is disturbing me."

"Oh! 'got your point.Extreme love and affection causes suspicion and doubts.Your attachment to him,your sentiments for him are not allowing you to let him be away but you know Indian ladies and wives are known for helping their consorts and never be hurdle on their path.I want you to remember that."

"I remember every thing what all you have taught me and that's why I did not become an impediment on his way but unfortunately I am not able to dispel away premonitions what I am getting with me.I can only pray God and leave everything to my fate."

" That is good.To-morrow morning before he leaves,we will go to our village deity,pray her with all our traditional rituals,invoke her blessings and bring PRASADAM for the well being of Sanatan and give that to him."
"Yes,that will be good."

Roshani got up very early next morning,she finished her morning routine and took bath.She was ready with all stores required for the worship of the deity before her mother got up.It was astonishing to see her got up so early and ready for going to temple.Mother hurriedly got ready and they both went to the temple. Priest of the temple was surprised to see them so early and got panicky to imagine something unknown,however, they told him that there was nothing to worry for him,however,they wanted an elaborate pooja of the deity.Adopting the detailed traditional rituals,priest performed all the pooja which took over an hour after which with the plate of prasadam they straight came to the residence of Sanatan who was almost ready to proceed on his journey.

"Sanatan ,you know that I have always treated you as my son but unfortunately you did not like to bid adieu to me before leaving this village and all of us," said the mother.

"I am sorry.I extremely regret for hurting your feelings but I had already expressed to Roshani that I had no courage to face you and my mission is such that I can't stop myself.But only I request you to pray God,so that I come back,marry her and settle down as a normal family man."

" My prayers and blessings will always be there with you but I also don't know,why something though unknown is disturbing me."

" It is your love to me which makes you worried but you need not get disturbed I will come back just in a couple of years and will always be in touch with Roshani.See I am not vacating this room,I am just going with my clothing and daily use items."

" Ok,may God,always be with you.But please be continuously in touch with us otherwise I may not be able to control

Roshani.She is extremely grieved and I doubt she may not remain in her senses."
"Worry not,she is everything to me and I will not allow her to be in tears."

Sanatan took leave of them and marched on his way ahead.Roshani remained looking at him.gradually his figure sitting in the jeep went on reducing in size and ultimately disappeared from her eyes.With a heavy heart she accompanied her mother to come back home under the burden of dual anxiety of Sanatan on one hand and her father on the other.

Her father hardly in fifties was suffering for the last couple of years.He had developed some deformity in his skeleton system which the doctors available in the nearby small town were not able to diagnose and it was not possible for him to go to some big town and consult some renowned physician or surgeon. Sanatan who had developed some knowledge of homeopathy and biochemic system of medicines while living in that village with an aim to help poor people had been administering his medicines.some charity organization had arranged a camp in a nearby village whose doctors had examined him and advised certain medicines along with calcium and vitamin D3 supplements.whatever,amount of medicines which had been received from that organization was being given to him.Though there had been improvement but still he was confined to his house premises.he was the only bread winner of the family and his sickness had put the entire family in precarious condition and that was the most difficult period for the family.As a godsend Sanatan had helped them in many ways and that had brought them too close though he already had a high reputation of goodwill and had been visiting them earlier also.

Roshani tried to keep herself busy in house hold activities to divert her mind from the agony and pains of his departure.The summer vacations were half way through and the exam results were expected in coming few days and that was another source of anxiety.She had made a promise to Sanatan that she would not stop her studies under any circumstances until she became a graduate and that was also giving another dimension to her worries but let what may,she would keep up the promise.the family condition was not still out of the woods though she was getting some money through adult literacy classes which had been started as a result of efforts made by Sanatan under the auspices of the state government and also through some other tutorial classes,however,that was just a pittance.her mother had learnt tailoring work and she had started stitching clothes using the stitching machine received through state government which was also fetching some money.family had a small farm land where her father used to grow vegetables and different varieties of melons.Though that was seasonal but still that was more profitable being cash crop but that income had also stopped due to his sickness.

The first Saturday evening when she received the telephone call from

Sanatan,her happiness had bounced by leaps and bounds and she had felt him very close to her forgetting that he was at a very far off place.

"How is your life and missionary work going on in your new place,?"Asked Roshani.

"As long as Roshani(light) is there in my life,nothing can stop me from my target.I am just starting my work but I have to repeat the same exercise what all I had done at your place.Here also everything is new," replied Sanatan.

"How are the people there and how do they behave?"

"That is the million dollar question.As such they appear very simple but they are not so open as I had found people in your place."

"Then how are you going to handle them?"

"I will first win their confidence with my intent,behavior and actions and then try to do whatever I can do within the period of two years as assured to you."

"Oh,good remember that."

He had long discussion with Roshani's mother and father as well.That reassured them of his commitment towards Roshani and whatever apprehensions might had cropped up in their mind vanished.

The time was passing with the memories of the bygone days and waiting for the phone calls from Sanatan on every Saturdays.A period of three weeks lapsed that exam results were declared and Roshani had stood a first   division in the higher secondary exams conducted by the state board.While that raised her morale,the urge for higher studies became stronger.College facilities were not available in the nearby area and the nearest government post graduate degree college available for girls was quite far off in the bigger town and the only option to continue her further studies was to reside at the college hostel.

The next Saturday when the telephone call was received from Sanatan,without wasting any moment Roshani quickly added,

"I have got first division in my higher secondary exams,are you happy?"

" Oh! so good.I am delighted to know of that.Keep your promise to become a graduate."

" Definitely.But you know many problems are there which create hindrance."

" Don't worry,I will arrange some finance for you and also you will get the scholarship meant for students of downtrodden communities. Likewise you can manage."

" Ok.I will do.How are the things there now?"

" I am able to make good rapport with some elders of the tribal communities,they are appreciating my mission and getting inclined to help me."

" Very good.Mother goddess will always help you.Will you tell me,why did you chose that area to venture when you were doing so well here in this area and I was also quite close to you."

" I have already spent ten years in your area and enough work has been done but this is an area where things are still in bad shape and then I am here only for a couple of years."

" But why did you chose that area?"

"There is some very special reason but I will tell you later."

" Very often we hear of something wrong going on in that area which worries us,keep your safety first."

" You are right.Here I avoid to move on foot,I prefer to use my jeep.I know that people here are unpredictable as they lack confidence & faith in any body but once they believe in some body they develop unquestionable blind faith."

" My mother wants to send you some home made sweets ,would you like that?"

" Why do you ask that.I always like the sweet items prepared by your Mummy.Definitely send me that without any second thought."

" Anything else you want."

" No thanks.Ok ,good bye."

The discussions were over but they had given a lot of thoughts to Roshani to worry for and she was at a loss to decide whether to pressurize him to come back or allow him to do what all he was doing at his new place.

CHAPTER.II- The Clue.

"Baba I am here to serve you and your people,nobody has called me,nobody has sent me and no body is paying me anything and also I am not going to get any benefit of being here in this difficult place.Already three months are over and you might have observed and seen what am I trying to do for your people,then why do you doubt me?"Said Sanatan to the eldest person of the community of that village.

"My heart asks me to believe you but my mind says other way round and also most of the people of the community and village are having many an apprehensions and therefore I am searching my soul."Replied the old man.

"But why are you having so much of doubt in me."

"There are enough reasons for that and we are having many bitter experiences of the past which do not allow us to believe in any body."

"Can you tell me some of them?"
"We have Many bad experiences in the past but definitely I will share with you some of them which have happened during past twenty years and which most of the people of present generation have seen themselves.The most recent experience is that,
about five years ago a Christian priest came to this village and started living in a hut in a corner of the village.He was extremely polite,well behaved and helpful and was living a very simple life like other villagers.Gradually he became very popular amidst all the villagers and practically a helper of all of us and people developed unquestionable faith in him.After an year or so he requested us for a small plot of land to get a small shrine- a place of worship constructed for him.We gave him a small piece of barren land and he got a small shrine made with the help of village people and some hired tabours.After a few months passed by,we observed that some people started coming to his hut and the shrine and some activities started going on there.After another one year had passed

by that their gathering in the place of their worship became regular & intense and they began preaching their religion in the village and offering doles for converting our villagers to their religion.These activities went up by and by and in a time span of five years they got a large number of people of our village and nearby villages converted to their religion,however,without changing their names and without giving any official change of their original religion so that those converts looked as if they were holding their original religion,caste and community and in government parlance they would continue to avail the facilities of reservation and other things.The conversion became like an epidemic and scores and scores of people got converted to Christianity.The facilities and benefits as promised to converts were given in the beginning but afterwards they were left to their fate thereby vanishing the illusion.A few years back another group of people came who asked the converts to go back to their original religion and insisted for reconversion back.In this process there were a lot of scuffles and violence and

ultimately the group pleading for reconversion back to their original religion was successful and the shrine of priests erected on our plot of land was also converted to the shrine of our deity.The entire happenings left behind a very bad taste of things to us and to-day any one like a priest or religious leader is seen,we try to keep him at bay."
"Oh ! so very bad.Actually nobody should play with the religious sentiments of any one."

That was really something unpleasant and unwelcome.But any way don't worry I have nothing to do with any religion or anything like that.Will you tell me some other instance which hurts you most.

" Several years back a couple had come to us in guise of social activist.They were putting up in a nearby town and were coming to our village and nearby villages and doing a lot of good things,telling us about   health   & hygiene,cleanliness,eradication of caste considerations and about upliftment of

women folk.After an year or so they started organizing classes for women and grown up girls and teaching them.That effort was highly appreciated.Gradually they started telling grown up girls so many things of modern systems,fashion and modern living.That worried us but we did not mind much.A couple of years passed by and we noticed that some grown up girl would suddenly vanish from some function or assembly or gathering of our community.We made our own searches but nothing was coming through.Months would pass and the girl would not come back.That worried us but we had no courage to contact police or civil authorities.One day a gentleman like you came who took us to police station and lodged first information report and started searching for our missing girls.It took about an year or so that we came to know that the couple whom we had believed so much was involved in human trafficking and our girls had been allured,taken away and put into various prohibited activities.With the help of that gentleman after a couple of years we could get back a few of our girls but still nothing is known about several girls.This had been our most horrible experience which has jolted our faith and belief in any outsider."

" What do you think about the person who helped rescue your girls?"

" He was a perfect gentleman whom we treated like a god.He remained with us for about three to four years but suddenly disappeared one day and never came back.I don't know what happened to him."

"Can you tell me something about him?"

"He was a tall,fair colored good looking person,wearing a golden frame spectacle,having bare forehead and was very soft spoken.He looked like a Bengali gentleman but whenever,enquired he did not tell much about himself."

"Can you tell me his name?"

"As I remember, we used to call him as Sadaa Babu and possibly his name was Sadananad Sarkar."

Sanatan felt as if he had fallen from heavens to the earth,his eyes got filled with tears and he felt his throat having got choked.He could not control himself and was not able to talk any further.The old man was surprised to see his condition and was wonder struck that why had he become like that just by listening the name Sadanad Sarkar.

Sanatan just left the place without speaking even a word,hurriedly came back to his jeep,started the vehicle and moved away somewhere in the opposite direction of that village.The behavior of Sanatan had created a stir in the mind of the old man and he could guess that there was some shocking effect or may be electrifying effect in the name of Sadaa Babu which had caused some uncontrollable effect in the young man but what exactly had happened to him was far from his speculation.

The old man remembered his first meeting with Sadaa Babu.It was an afternoon of a summer month,the sun was still radiating heat & throwing fire balls and it was beyond any body's liking to get out of the house.He was sitting wearing just a loin cloth in his verandah on a very old rope oven bamboo cot the ropes of which were sunk deep down below.The verandah was also just a bamboo structure covered with a roof made of dry leaves.Though entire set up was quite primitive but it was reasonably cool & comfortable.Suddenly he saw a middle aged man coming to his hut.The man appeared tired of sun heat and his face looking perched and the body sweating profusely.He had a wide forehand,his face was still glowing despite tiredness writ large on the face.He was wearing a white dhoti and white kurta,having a golden frame spectacle on his nose and a cloth bag hanging on his left shoulder.He came to him and asked,

"Baba ! I am very tired. Can I get a glass of water and relax in your hut for a while?"
"But who are you and what makes you come here?"
"I am Sadanad. I am a social worker and I am moving from village to village."
"But I don't know you,how can I allow you to relax here in my hut, however,I will give you water and you can quench your thirst."
"Thank you Baba."

Sadanad sat on the ground,stretching his both the legs,possibly giving some relief and respite to them.Old man gave him an earthen bowl full of water which Sadanand held with his both the hands and drank hurriedly.He was so tired that he could not lift up himself and just spread himself on the ground and within a few minutes slept there itself on the bare ground.The old man found himself in dilemma to wake him up or let him sleep as such but some element of merciful consideration prevailed in him and he allowed him to sleep there.A time span of over a couple of hours elapsed that the evening started knocking at the doors and the old man got worried.He shook him and asked him to wake up and go. Sadanand slowly opened his eyes but he was not in a position to get up,however,on continuous insistence of the old man some how he got up but still he was so tired that his body was not supporting him to get up and move.He very humbly requested the old man to allow him to be there in the night and positively next early morning he would move away.

"See,you are thrusting yourself upon me.I had clarified you in the beginning itself that you can get water only but seeing your plight I allowed you to sleep for sometimes.Now better you go."

"Baba,I will not make myself a burden on you.I don't want any thing,only because I was feeling sick and tired I could not stop myself sleeping over here.Please don't feel annoyed,I will go and sleep somewhere beneath a tree."

"Don't you have a place of your stay?"

"I have a place but that is quite far off.Every day early morning I leave my place with some eatables and go to a pre-selected village where I meet people,understand their problems and try to help them and return back in the evening.This routine continues till I am able to take some care of them."

"Then why did you not do that to-day?"

"I was in a nearby village where I have been working for a month and have been well versed with their problems.I thought of coming to this village to make my next field of activity."

"Then you should have come early and gone back early."

"Baba, you are right.I was not feeling well for the last couple of days but without worrying for that I have been doing my work.To-day I was feeling too weak but still I came out but unfortunately there was no energy left in my body and my legs betrayed me to move further.Any way God is great,He will help me.Thank you Baba,I will go somewhere,find a tree and sleep beneath that."

"No,no,I did not mean that.In fact,so many things we have seen that we are hesitant to believe in any one unless we have tried and tested him and you are totally new here for any one of us."

"You are right.As much I have seen you people,you are very simple and clear hearted and may be due to that some people would have cheated you,but believe it every body is not same ."

"Ok,let me see."

The old man permitted him to stay,however,with the condition that whatever is offered he would eat that which

Sadanand happily accepted.The old man went to the nearby house and came back after a few minutes and asked him to ease himself and get freshened up during next half an hour's time.he brought a small lamp,filled it with some oil,commandeered a match stick and lit the same.A weak light emanated from the lamp and possibly that was enough for him and might be similar light was enough for the people of the village as well.he offered him a little bigger earthen bowl full of water and directed him to go to fields to ease himself. Sadanand followed the instructions and went outside as by then he had become accustomed of such situations though in the beginning of his venture he had found such a situation very difficult and beyond his comprehension.He came back after fifteen twenty minutes and cleaned his hands using ashes of burnt dried cow dung which was the normal practice in most of the villages and also washed his legs and feet.Some village people came with mats and edibles in their hands.Two small mats were spread on the ground on whom he and the old man sat side by side.Disc like plates made of dry leaves were placed before them on which rice and some curry was served to them.the old man took some water in his right hand,sprinkled that around the food,folded his both the palms and prayed something after which he asked him to start eating the meals.though extremely simple,it was very tasty which Sadanand took merrily.while they were taking the meals he heard some feeble voice of women singing in a nearby house. He could not understand the words but the sound was quite melodious.after the dinner was over the singing stopped.he casually asked the old man,

"when we were taking the meals there was some sweet voice of singing of women,what was that ?"
"That is our custom that when some guest takes his meals women of the house of host sing in his honor.I am here alone,our meals were prepared and served by my neighbor who are grand children of my elder brother."
"Oh! so nice. In my childhood I had seen such a system in some villages and

families of Uttar Pradesh also.In fact my mother's younger sister was married in a good family in that region and I remember to have gone there twice or thrice and there also I had noticed such a system but as I grew up such things were not there."

"That is how,we differ from others.We are trying to keep our traditions and customs alive but I apprehend how long this may be there."

"I will suggest that let customs & traditions continue undisturbed simultaneously with the growth and development of time changes should also come.You people must become literate and well educated and adopt good practices of health & hygiene but culture which is unique and your identity need not be disturbed."

"We are very apprehensive.Many people came to us in the previous years who promised us good life but they cheated us and misused our goodness.If that is the effect of modernization and progress,we don't want that.We are very happy the way we are."

"No doubt you are correct in your observations and experiences but I hope

that will change.Good people have always been more on the earth than the bad people.Let me also try,definitely you all will realize that."
"Ok,ok."

The old man asked him to relax and more of talks could be there in coming days.Two young persons brought a bamboo cot which was also in quite dilapidated condition. They spread a thick sheet like thing made of old clothes and readied it for him to sleep. He thanked them and spread himself over the bed to sleep.Being unwell and tired he went into sleep immediately.Next morning he woke up early in the morning feeling reasonably refreshed.A few minutes after him,the old man also woke up who was sleeping a little away from him and he asked him to go out to the fields to ease himself. Both took bowls of water in their hands and went towards the fields at two different places.They came back after half an hour's time and by then the sky was becoming clearer and clearer heralding the arrival of dawn.The old man arranged water for washing of his hands and then he was offered a small twig of Acacia to use as tooth brush and clean his teeth & mouth.He had earlier used twigs of Neem(Nimba) tree which were very good and refreshing but it's bristles were not very soft,however,he found Acacia twig giving very very soft bristles and was also quite refreshing.That was some new experience which gave him a lesson.

He was then taken to a nearby well where an youth of the village offered him a big pitcher full of water using which he took bath and wiped off his body with a cloth offered by the youth.He changed a few clothes which were available in his bag and cleaned his undergarments and spread the cleaned clothes for drying on a rope tied between two trees. He took some water in his hands and looking towards Sun god,he prayed him and then dropped the same on the ground.He came back to the place where he had stayed overnight and sat on the cot.

He felt awry to see the behavior of the person who was not ready to allow him to relax some hours back when he was too tired was then showering so much of consideration on him but he stood obliged to all the care that he had received at the hands of his new host.He thanked them profusely and wanted to move away but he was asked to stay for some more time,have his breakfast with them and then go wherever he wanted. However,he apprised them that his rendezvous was their own village,which he wanted to make his field of activity.A person offered himself to accompany him to the whole village to help him familiarize with the people and problems of the village and it's inhabitants.He agreed to that but still some iota of suspicion existed in both the parties, he thinking whether the help offered was genuine and the people of the old man having an idea to cross check the authenticity of the intentions of that person new to the village.

CHAPTER.III- The Remembrances.

"I don't believe in death-bed philosophy,for me every new day is a precious gift of God! almighty and that is given for doing something good to every one who is needy and is suffering."Said Sanatan to Roshani.

"Then why don't you help me first.I need that most.You are wandering here and there going from one place to another helping people,educating them and trying to give succor to those who are in pains,but you ignore me."

"How can it be,for me you are equally precious gift of God,given exclusively to me.But I always apprehend what will be our end,where shall our story lead to?"

"It is your nature and still you say,you don't have death-bed philosophy.What else will be death-bed philosophy.Be optimist,enjoy the present,don't fret for future but remain determined and committed to your goal.That is what has been taught to me and I stand by that.I have already made my stand clear.The next turn is yours."

"I know that, but remember I have done every possible thing for your village,your

people and of course to you.This year you will pass your higher secondary exam and will move to graduation.I am sanguine that one day you will do something great and become an identifiable personality."

"I know,I know that you always encourage me but as a person I need something else which only you can give me."

"Whatever,I have that is yours.Remember the story of Lord Buddha.When as an enlightened personality he came back to Kapilvastu,he met his parents and thereafter he met his wife Yashodhara.She was in tears and could make only few exchanges with The Lord but when He was ready to go back,she brought their son Rahul who was by then an adolescent and asked Him to give His son His inheritance.Lord Buddha immediately asked one of His disciples to bring a begging bowl,gave that to Rahul,made him a Buddhist monk and took him to accompany Him.Though in a very small measure but I have also become like that and who knows a similar may be my legacy to you."

" No,no.I am not interested in that.I had a very tough and difficult life from the very day I came to this earth.I want to have your company to have a settled life in your parental place and yet serve the people in our own humble way."

"I wish and pray God !that He may bestow upon you all His blessings but you know,future is unknown.We can wish something but what would ultimately come out is in the hands of supreme being."

"To-day,I find you showing split and fatalistic attitude which frightens me.Are you having some premonitions?"

"No,no.Nothing like that.In fact I am struggling with myself. Heart is asking me not to go to the place I have planned to go but mind is asking me to go ahead and concentrate on the job which is there in my mind."

"But what is that to which your mind is pressurizing you so much that you are having your own internal conflict.Why don't you tell me.I may be of some help to you."

"See,my father after the sudden death of my mother had become totally detached from the world and he had practically *forgotten me also.He was a very religious and chaste person.His relatives and friends tried their best to bring him back to normal life even by reminding to fulfil the dreams which he had for me but he could not reconcile.At length somebody suggested him to go to some undeveloped & Interior place of the country and dedicate himself to the service of forlorn and helpless people.This suited him and he deposited enough money for my studies and left the home to such a place and dedicated himself serving the people.Regularly he was in touch with me and continuously encouraging me to look sharp to my goal which I achieved also but suddenly I found his call missing.I was badly disturbed but kept myself busy with my studies and secured a position in the list of selected candidates in the civil services also but without him I was finding myself miserable.I decided to find him out and at length joined this organization.I have been to several places but could not locate him.To divert my attention I was sent here and fortunately I got myself so engrossed that I totally forgot everything else but sometimes back I had a dream in which my father indicated towards that place and wanted to tell me something but I was so happy in the dream that I woke up to meet him but found myself alone and nobody else was there.Since then idea came to my mind to go to that place and find out about my father. My charity organization has also endorsed my proposal to go there and work for the people the way I have done here.But when every thing is ready I am having a conflict in my mind as my heart is not permitting me to leave you."*

"Oh! so that is the reason.Alright I will never come on your way,you decide what your conscience permits and I will be fully with you. "

He remembered the above discussions,one day he had with Roshani to convince her of leaving her place to come to that new destination.It was a very dark night and outside it was horrible,raining cats and dogs with intermittent lightning thunders and dreaded sounds of winds slapping   against the doors and windows which could tremble even the most hard hearted man and in such a situation living alone in a room of a house which was having a bad reputation was a tough job. He was wandering in the limitless sky of remembrances which were moving very fast before the screen of his mind that the memory of Roshani came and halted in his mind.The memory of his lady love was so intense that he was continuously repenting of having left her in a far off place but his desire to know,where was his father and if he had died,then answer to know how had he died was equally intense and he was sure to find the truth somewhere in that place.He had got a hint from the old man that his father had been in that area and was doing something for the unprivileged people but where was he was still far behind the cloud nine.

The dread of that night had enveloped so much so that his mind was also getting darkened but the thunder flash of lightening was occasionally making such a light that for a flash of a second every thing was getting lighted & becoming visible. Though thunder sound was shaking the heart and body but that flash of light was giving him so many thoughts & memories.suddenly he remembered of his meeting with octogenarian professor whom he had met while working in the desert area and who was so highly impressed with his dedication & devotion that he agreed to teach him the occult science of seeing in the candle flame piercing through the expanse of time of the events which may be lying in the womb of future.He decided to use that knowledge to locate and find out his father when the weather conditions became normal and he was able to control himself to concentrate in that endeavor.That thought kindled in him a new spark burning away other disturbing thoughts and he slept for rest of the night.Though the inclement weather continued for a few days but the dreadful nights vanished.

Several days and nights passed by that gradually the things improved.Days became sunny and nights became clearer and the lunar cycle came into the night sky.It was a Thursday night that he made up his mind to use the science of seeing the future of events.He came back from his work quite early in the evening,cleaned himself,took bath and by dusk sat before the photo of his deity for worship and meditation.After an hour's meditation he found himself able to concentrate for the job.He took a big candle,commandeered a match and with the flame of the burning match stick lit the wick of the candle.He placed the candle on a wooden plank and started seeing through the burning flame.As he concentrated deep and deeper a hazy look of horizon appeared before his eyes which gradually became clearer and clearer.He saw his father working for the good of people for a moment and then disappeared,however,after sometimes he saw a person,a middle aged person who appeared to have been very close to his father and he wanted to tell him something and thereafter suddenly everything disappeared from the zone of flame.Sanatan could recognize very clearly the face of the person whom he saw in the flame and also got the meaning of unheard message.This clue was enough for him to continue his search.

Next morning Sanatan was invigorated and exalted.he got himself readied very early and set out to go to all the villages he had been so far and meet every person and possibly out of them he might be able to find out the face which he had seen in the candle flame.he decided to cover a minimum of two villages each day.Though the job was big but he had lost the sense of tiredness and seemed to be in a hurry to complete his search mission.Five days were spent,he had covered ten villages and met people in all the houses but still there was no success which was dampening his hopes but he was fighting against hopes.Another five days past,another set of ten villages covered yet no outcome.He had enquired from different old and knowledgeable people about Sadaa Babu,they all had confirmed that they knew him but no body was able to tell regarding his whereabouts and where was he then.One very old and frail person from a far off village advised him to contact Biru

Mahato who was always escorting Sadaa Babu as his shadow and he may be located in the coming village fair after a week.That gave a sense of satisfaction to Sanatan.

"Excuse me; are you Biru Mahato?"

Sanatan moved in the fair from one end to other and from one corner to another and moved to every nook & corner but the face which he had seen in the candle flame was nowhere in sight and the evening was approaching due to which many men,women and children having come from far off villages had started returning back to their homes. Though fair was to continue next day also as many young boys & girls were interested to be in GHOTUL for choosing soul mates for each other and subsequently marry them.Suddenly in the corner of a sweet shop he noticed a man whose face was resembling with the face he remembered to have seen in the candle flame.Without wasting even a moment he rushed to him and enquired about him.

"No,I am not Biru Mahatao,how do you know him?"

"Sorry,extremely sorry.The face that I remember is exactly matching with that of yours and that brought me to you."

"Will you tell me ,why you want Biru Mahato and does he know you."

"No,neither he knows me nor I know him ,but I need him."

"But ,what for,you don't seem to be from this area?"

"Yes,I am not a man of this area.I need his help and only he can help me."

"What is that specific work."

"I am searching for my father who had been in this area for several years and Biru Mahato was very close to him."

"Who was your father?"

"Sadanad Sarkar,popularly known as Sadaa Babu."

That man jumped up with joy and his response and reaction became totally changed.He stood up and hugged him and with a sense of some invisible relief said,

"I know,I am the Biru Mahato.Are you his son?"

" Yes.I am his son and the only son.I have been searching for my father here & there for several years but without result.Here I came to serve the people and also find out my father and to know what had happened to him and also to complete the job whatever he had left undone".

"Ok.I will help you.Would you mind staying here with me in the night? When the commotion and bustle of the activities are over I will tell you everything that I know".

"No problem.I am ready to stay but can you help me arrange some place for stay and bedding etc?"

"You need not worry.You are son of a selfless great man,I will take care of you."

Biru Mahato had made reasonably good arrangement of his dinner and stay in a make shift tent,however,he himself had gone to attend some program.It was a very pleasant night,cool breeze blowing across the whole fair area and moon shining in the sky spreading the soothing radiance on the earth which was weaving an endless canopy of visible threads over the entire environ.beneath that celestial canopy some people were camping in make shift tents,some under the shady trees and also some in open ground around burning dry logs.The whistling of wind was producing a melody,a sweet melody,a melody of tranquility & blessedness. Sanatan got swept away in thoughts of divine bliss and was amazed to feel how happy those undeveloped people were amidst the scanty & paucity dwelling upon the heaps of dearth of everything which a developing or developed man wants.he looked to the moon shining up above in the sky and got himself lost in the thought that from the beginning of the universe the moon was endlessly spreading coolness,smoothness and pious ness on the earth and yet there was lack of its soothing effect on the human lust & desires.Though stirred-up deep in his thoughts yet he was feeling so light&relaxed as if he had found his father alive and was walking with him.The chain of his thoughts got broken when he saw scattered lights emanating through burning small lamps,it was only at one place that he noticed a petromax burning which was throwing away a shining light covering over a vast area.Probably some entertainment program was going on over there.Suddenly he heard some sweet sound emanating from some unfamiliar musical instrument accompanied with sound of beating of drums.Though he enjoyed and relished the music but liked to know where from same was emanating and what was the instrument which was producing that unfamiliar sweet melody.Gradually sleep took him over and he slept.

Next morning when he woke up Biru Mahato was already present there with a bowl of tea which he offered to him.He took the bowl thankfully and slowly finished the tea.Biru asked him to accompany him to go out for easing himself.He finished his morning routine the way village people used to do and took his bath at a make shift arrangement. Biru took him at a shop where fresh sweets and savories were being cooked and he asked him to take items of his choice.He took Jalebi(a sweet made of fine flour and jaggery) and some salt items and a glass of goat milk.Having finished their breakfast Biru took him to another place.There was a very big hut where a lot of things and instruments were lying kept haphazardly. Sanatan was surprised to see an strange environment and asked Biru,

" this hut looks to be quite peculiar,what is that ?"

"There was GHOTUL here last night."

"What is the significance of GHOTUL.?"

"There are certain very old customs and traditions in our villages and GHOTUL is most famous of them.You would have heard that in olden times there was a system of SWAYAMVAR (Self selection of groom) amongst the high society girls and princesses,a crude & community form of the same prevalent in our area is GHOTUL.The boys and girls of marriageable age adorned in their traditional attire and ornaments come to the annual fair,they meet with each other;they dance, play games,enjoy various events in the fair and during nights collectively meet here and select their life partners.Their parents and relatives gather

and solemnize wedding ceremony.During ceremony many types of entertainment programs,music& dance and collective dinner is arranged.In some cases when parents are not present,marriages are fixed and solemnized later on deciding some suitable & auspicious occasion.You can see several very unfamiliar items,they are our musical instruments."

"During night I heard a very sweet& melodious sound ,however,such a sound I have not heard earlier.Could you tell me something?"

Biru took him to an instrument and said, "See this instrument.It is made of a special type of bamboo,a long straight bamboo piece.It is very hard to blow this instrument and only some experienced person who can blow air with pressure for a long time can produce sound from it but the sound is very unique and very sweet. This is a must for wedding ceremonies and you might have heard the same last night."

"What is that ,this instrument known as?"

"This is Naad Murali(great flute)."

"The boys and girls who meet in GHOTUL,are they acquainted of each other earlier or they meet in the fair for the first time?"

"Mostly,they meet for the first time.Day long,they remain here in the fair and participate in various activities which brings them closer to each other.They talk and discuss about each other and ultimately decide to marry or not but once they marry,they are committed to each other for the whole life."

"It seems to be a very good system and is devoid of many evils prevailing in the civil societies.I hope this system is still existing the way it has been there from earlier times."

"No,it had been changed and there your father had played very important role."

"What was that,what did my father do?"

"The system of GHOTUL was basically meant only for our own boys and girls and all our communities were observing unwritten ethics & code of conduct very religiously but gradually some outsiders started purchasing some village chieftains and started participating in GHOTUL.We

came to know that they were alluring our girls and misusing them and clandestinely taking them away in name of marriage and using them for flesh trade.Your father while working in our area noticed this evil and he worked hard to eradicate the evil.At that point of time many people of our area and community did not co-operate with him and rather opposed him but later on they realized what good he was doing for us."

"What all did my father do,will you please tell me more about his work?"

"Don't be in a hurry.Gradually I will tell you many things but let me know,what is your purpose of knowing those things and what makes you come to our area?

"I am here also to serve you all and in fact I have been serving unprivileged people for several years and simultaneously I am searching for my father also but I could not know about him.It is only prudence of luck that somebody told me about you.I am very serious to know if he is alive and if so why did he not contact me and in case he is no more how did he die and who did his last rites?"

"Oh! I can understand your worry and fully share your pains.I will be with you wherever and whenever you want me and worry not whatever was required had been done."

Though Biru Mahato did not tell him all the details of what had happened to his father but he was able to make out that his father was no more and possibly Biru Mahato had done all his last rites.He felt extreme gratitude to Biru but that sparked his anxiety more intensely to know that how did his father die and why did he not convey his last words to him?

Sanatan requested Biru to be with him and help him the way he had been doing to his father as he was very keen to peruse the work his father had been doing.He took the contact details of Biru and with a heavy heart took leave of him and went away.

CHAPTER.IV-The Pain

Biru Mahato,no doubt,avoided straight reply to Sanatan to tell him about what had happened to his father but he had no control over his own memories which had been recorded in the hard disc of his mind.He was swinging forward and backward in the memory lane with many flashes coming to him and disappearing leaving behind the trail of agonies & pains and also joy of happy moments but ,whenever,he remembered of the end of story that was extremely painful and that too remembering that he had to act as closest relative to perform his funeral rites,a person whom he adorned and always treated a crusader.In fact he had tried his best to forget the things and usher in a new time frame to restart his life being detached from the good and evils of life around him but the unexpected meeting of Sanatan had stirred in him and churned his emotions from deep inside.

He was sweeping across the tide of time which had become a part of eternity.Suddenly a flash appeared before his mind that he was a helpless creature,a forlorn wandering aimlessly having lost his own identity that one day he met a gentleman who was fair looking,middle aged & bespectacled person selflessly helping and serving the people who asked him in a voice full of compassion & affection,

"Why are you looking so morose and sunk in pains?"
"It has become a part of my life."He had replied with anguish.
" You are an young man,this is not the age to be like that."
"But my destiny has betrayed me and I find vacuum all around me"
"I feel,destiny is an alibi for those who have no faith in their own self. You don't appear to be that kind of a man."
"Definitely,I have been a person full of life but God was unkind to me and now I have lost charm of life."

"See,I am like your father,could you tell me something that torments you.Possibly I may be of some help go you."

Biru looked at the gentleman from top to toe.He was not inclined to open out himself and liked to contain his agony to himself but the affectionate radiance on the face of the gentleman was inviting him to tell the truth & lighten himself but still he was hesitant.He again heard the gentle voice,

"I find you in some conflict with yourself.Don't hesitate, tell me whatever,pains you have I will try my best to soothe you."

Biru could not resist himself any more and he came out in a voice full of pains,

"My father was very proficient in making the artifacts which had great demand.When I was a child I had seen some people coming from outside periodically and taking away those stores.But they were paying very meager

amount,yet we were happy.After my studies I also joined my father and started learning his art & craft and helping him.He wanted to make me better than himself.One day while coming back from a Haat (village market) I saw some of those traders going back from our village after having purchased our items.I heard them talking that they were making a big profit out of our items and also discussing of a shop where they were selling those items.I came back home and told my father of the same and wanted myself to go to that shop and sell my items at a reasonable price.My father agreed.

After some days I went to the city,enquired about that store and met its owner and placed before him my proposal.He happily greeted my proposal which was going to be mutually beneficial to both of us.Thereafter,our destiny changed and I also learnt the traits of the trade along with skill which my father was giving me.By and by I told other villagers also to adopt the same practice but that invited wrath of *unscrupulous middleman who had been looting us.*

One night when I had gone out to some other village for attending a folk program where I stayed overnight.Next morning when I came back I found a very ghastly sight at my home.My father and mother were lying dead in a pool of blood and the whole house had been ransacked and all things of craft were lying broken & scattered.Police came and did all legal formalities.Villagers told me that last night a group of Naxalites had attacked our house and killed my parents & damaged all our belongings.The death of my father and mother totally shattered me and I felt myself as an orphan & an aim-less individual.My village people and my relatives helped me and I did all the funeral rites of my parents.However,such a departure of my parents created a hollow,a void in my life and all the enthusiasm & charm with which my life used to bubble vanished.Gradually relatives & others went their way back and I was left alone.One question was haunting me,why did

Naxalites attack only my house?My parents were very simple people and I was also keeping myself limited to my work.We were not at all involved in any activity that somebody from any group may be inimical to us.After some days having passed off,I came to know that those middlemen who were making huge profits out of us had arranged the attack and I was their target but due to prudence of luck I was not there when the attack was planned & executed.

I am wandering since then in search of solace and have been to many places but I did not get peace of mind anywhere.Some people suggested me to marry and restart life but whenever,I go back to my house memories of my parents haunts me and I feel myself a cause of their tragic death."

"Oh ! so sad.I can understand and feel the agony,the pain and the anguish that you may have and I am sanguine I will be able to help you and take you out of the situation you are in now."
"But how? You don't look to be a saint or Mahatama or Sanyasi,you just look to be a

simple man like me,then how shall you help.I have already met many such people and they could do nothing ."

"You have recognized me a simple man,you are a simple man and when two simple persons meet,they can do wonders & miracles.You join me and I will see that you forget the agony."

"Ok.I accept your proposal.What should I do next?"

"You are just like my son,you do whatever I say and after some days you will yourself realize what your life needs.Now let us go to your house where you lived with your parents."

Biru though unwilling yet took Sadaa Babu to his parental home.It was a small house with walls and surroundings kept well clean,neat & tidy,however,most of the house hold items were still lying scattered and floors being dirty as if things had been left the way they were ransacked. Sadaa Babu himself came forward to clean the things and rearranged them quickly as the darkness was descending down. Biru accompanied him and hurriedly made the things in order.Thereafter,arrangement was made for cooking of some food with whatever,was available inside the house.He asked Biru to ease out and himself also followed suit.They took the meals,washed themselves and the utensils and placed them in proper places. Biru took out two bamboo cots and placed them outside the house on whom they sat facing each other.

"The death is inevitable and is the ultimate truth of life.It is only the way,it came gives you calmness or remorse.I do agree that your parents met with a very unfortunate course of death but see the other side of it also.Had you been there,imagine what would have happened and in that case situation would have been totally different.Either your parents would have been left to suffer for their whole life or no body would have been there to know of your family.----
See, like you I have also suffered when my wife died,I had the darkness all around me.I lost the meaning of being on the earth and in dejection & desperation left my

house and am now roaming but helping the needy people.I have got a meaning to my life." Said Sadaa Babu to Biru.

"What had happened to you sir?" Asked Biru.
"I have had a very happy family consisting of myself,my wife and my son who is studying in the university.I have a reasonably large landed property which was fetching me enough money for supporting a very good life and also I was teaching in a local school.I had misfortune of losing my wife when it was not at all expected and I also had become like you.But on advice of some saintly persons I have adopted the life of serving the unprivileged people and in that pursuit I am here in this place.After being in this field I found that half of the world does not know how the other half lives.Every one feels his pains and problems to be Himalayan but when we go out and see the other side of humanity,only then realization comes what is the reality of life,what is the truth of life and how much is the pain that I had or I am

*having and how many others are in much
greater pains & agony and are helpless."*
*"Oh,my God.So you have also suffered like
me and know the pain of losing dearest
ones. Ok,I will do the way you want me to
do."*
*"Good.That is the spirit .That will show you
something you have not seen so far."*

Biru arranged two bed sheets which looked
to be very old though they were
clean,spread them on the cots and readied
them to sleep. Sadaa babu went into sleep
after a few minutes of his lying down but
Biru remained looking at the stars up
above in the sky,searching for his parents
somewhere in their midst but could not see
them anywhere.When he was at the verge
of disappointment on failing to see his
parents,a thought came to his mind that
what was that father like gentleman going
to show him which might change his
mental condition of sorrow and   agony
particularly when so many elders amongst
his relatives and village people could not
do that.

Next day they got up early and finished their usual morning routine. Sadaa Babu did his prayers as well. Biru brought some roasted black gram and a sweet solution made of jaggery which they took as breakfast.It was around eight thirty,nine O'clock morning and both of them were ready for further activity. Sadaa Babu told him,

"To-day,you be with me.We shall go to a nearby village and study the problems and pains of the residents.You observe the things carefully.If you are having roasted gram and solid jaggery or whatever,eatable take that in a bag and that will serve as our lunch."
"Ok."

Biru took some roasted gram,whatever,was available inside the house and jaggery balls and placed them in a cloth bag and held that in his hand.Sadaa Babu took his bag and hang that on his left shoulder and both marched on their journey to the nearby village.

The way Sadaa Babu was moving he could guess that he was well familiar with that place. Both of them were moving silently. After half an hour's of journey they reached the village.he went to the first house where Biru saw that,

Sadaa Babu was greeted by an old lady and he went inside the house where an old man was lying on a cot who was in very bad shape of sickness. Sadaa Babu made some warm water on a smoldering hearth.He took that water and asked Biru to help him.Both of them supporting from back lifted the old man,Sadaa Babu took a cloth,soaked that in water,squeezed the excess water and with that wiped clean the entire body of the old man,changed his clothes,gave him some medicines and thereafter some food items.Once the feeding was over,he took away the dirty clothes to a nearby well where Biru took out water in a metallic pitcher. Sadaa babu prepared dettol   solution in a small tub,soaked all clothes in that and washed them using a soap and spread them on a rope tied between two poles for drying.He came back to the house,arranged the things properly,gave some instructions to the old lady and then left out along with Biru.He went to other house where one child was in trouble,he helped him and took care of other family members.Similarly he covered nearly a dozen houses and attended to their problems.It was by then afternoon and Biru was feeling hungry but he could not see any sign of tiredness on the face of Sadaa Babu.That was quite amazing to him.

Biru casually asked him if they could relax for some times.He could guess the problem and took Biru to nearby school building where they sat under the shade of verandah.
Biru took out roasted gram from his bag and both of them started taking the same with jaggery balls.That served them as their lunch.They took some water,spread a thin towel like cloth on the floor and lied down to relax.About one hour passed by that Sadaa Babu rose up and asked Biru for the next rendezvous.They went to a big house in front of which beneath a big

Banyan tree some girls were sitting and waiting and a black board was lying placed in front of them. Sadaa Babu told Biru that these were girls above the third standard who were not going to regular schools,they were waiting for him to teach them.

"But there is a regular school where we have relaxed,why these girls are not
going there to receive their regular education?"Enquired Biru.
"Did you notice some thing there?"
"I found things were normal as per village standards."
"No.Everything is not normal.Some very important thing is missing."
"What is that? I did not notice any thing wrong."
"No.Something is wrong.There is no toilet facility available for girls and boys in that school or for that purpose in most of the schools.They go in open for easing out themselves.Boys can do whatever they like but girls as they grow up can't go in open even for urinating and that makes them leave their studies beyond third standard."

"Oh,my God! That never struck to my mind."

As they reached to the girls,they were greeted by those girls and after a small prayer the teaching started.those girls had been divided in different groups as per their standards and Sadda Babu gave relevant jobs to concerned groups and started guiding them.sometimes he used black board to explain the topics and problems which were little difficult.This continued for three hours.the girls went back to their houses and Biru and Sadaa Babu proceeded on their way back.Biru had very patiently observed what all and how had that been done by the gentleman and he could not resist himself from asking him something.

"To-day I have seen you continuously working from morning till evening and I saw your utmost concern for the girls then what else are you doing?"
"On one hand I have taken up with the state government & some welfare organizations to construct toilets in the

schools wherever girls are studying but even if toilets are constructed water supply is a big problem in absence of which those toilets would become meaningless.In the meantime in agreement with the district authorities I am voluntarily running these classes,however,these girls are shown admitted in the schools. At the end of the session they will appear for the exams and will cross over to the next higher standard.Thus their studies are continuing up to Standard eight,"

"That is a very noble cause.I will also join with you,higher classes you conduct,lower classes I will run."

"Thank you very much.Once you do this you will know,how much pleasure and satisfaction this will give to you."

"But how many are such places where you are doing this."

"Only two and you be with me at both the places."

"Are you having some fixed time and place for running these classes?"

"No.Depending on the availability of school premises and weather conditions and some other people helping us,we decide

but these girls are very co-operative and responsive. They are very keen on receiving education and do their best."
"Any problem from their parents?"
"So many.In the beginning when I raised this proposal,they were not ready to listen to me.But gradually as they observed me,they appreciated it and willingly came forward to get their daughters educated."
"Do you charge them some thing?"
"No.Not at all.I am doing this as a satisfaction to myself.In fact I am doing a service to myself and to no body else."
"I have never seen a man like you.I feel you will have the same affection for me as well."
"Why not."

Biru's village had approached,he asked him to go to his house and start a fresh life taking for granted his pledge to serve the cause of girl's education as a homage to the departed souls. Biru was very keen that he accompanied to his home but he thankfully declined and marched on way to his place of stay.

Next day onwards Biru became his partner in his activities and as the time passed by his life was totally transformed as he had got a meaning to himself and to his life.

CHAPTER.V-The Canvas.

Sanatan returned back to his place of stay but he was completely drained and had lost his spirit.His pains and agony had no bounds and that was the day when he really felt himself a worthless creature.He had seen the sudden demise of his mother and his father becoming hysterical and relinquishing the battle field of a normal life,however,they had not given him the quantum of pains what he got with the hidden message from Biru that everything as required,in name of last rites of his father,had been done.But still he was interested to know how had his father died & when did he meet with his end and Biru was the only vital link who could tell him the truth.He decided to continue his life as usual and give Biru enough time to unfold the truth of his father's death.

That night he could neither cook his meals nor go out to purchase some edibles and remained sinking and floating in the ocean of anxieties & wild thoughts and cursing the supreme deity for being unjust to him and his parents.he was not able to understand what wrong has he done that he had to lose his parents in most unexpected circumstances and himself had landed in a life which was totally awry to that planned for him by his parents.many memories of childhood days were pricking him and he was weeping and sobbing remembering his parents and the time which had become a dream for him.

He was a small child studying in fifth standard;being a very brilliant student he was an object of jealousy of several students of his village.one day while playing football in the school ground some students had deliberately hit him on his leg due to which he fell down and was seriously injured.School authorities had given him first aid and sent him back to his house.When he came back with bandaged leg,his mother had become panicky and called his father immediately to take him to the doctor who was five kilometers away in a small town.Mother remained continuously awake for three nights until his pain subsided and after his becoming normal she had accompanied his father to the school principal and had rebuked him for his act of negligence.Thereafter school authorities had become strict towards naughty students and he had been regularly taken care of by them.

Every exam he would stand first and his mother would encourage him to be someone exceptional and would bring clothes & gifts of his choice.In fact she was the driving force behind his success in studies and was the biggest source of his motivation and inspiration.After having become matriculate he was admitted in a district college which was quite far off from the village,then mother had decided to hire a rented accommodation and stay there to look after him.That was a very difficult period for his parents as mother was staying with him in the city and father was staying alone at the village taking care of himself,his farming & cultivation and also continuing his teaching activities.However,during college holidays they would come to village and stay with father for some days and also on some occasions father would come to city to give them money and other essential items and only those times would be the period of togetherness of the family.He took two years to pass his higher secondary exams and that was the period which gave him the most valuable experience of knowing the role which parents play in someone's life,the expanding world as one comes out of the village life and aspirations of growing age.During that period he had received dual teaching both at school and also through his mother.He was continuously under observation of his mother who would notice every moment of his activities and advise wherever he could go wrong and also taught how to face the evils of the world without getting involved in any vice.

He had passed higher secondary exams with flying colors and was slated to go for higher education in an university.One day his mother told his father,

"I want my son to compete in the Indian Civil Services exam and become an Indian Administrative Service (IAS)officer and serve the people of this country with dignity."
"No,no.I don't like that.IAS officers have to spend their life under corrupt politicians and act on their whims & fancies and as such they can't do any constructive work.I want my son to study higher & higher and become a renowned professor and researcher who can show light to coming generations."
"I have seen enough of you teaching boys and girls and what have you got at the end of your innings."
"I have moulded clay dough into toys,utensils and valuable pieces."
"What nonsense.None of them have ever remembered you or paid you their respect and like you there are thousands of teachers.An IAS officer,whatever may be,is a king and ultimately they rule the country.Honesty or dishonesty depends on

the individual and it has nothing to do with any service or cadre.Why do you forget that a number of your students are politicians and a couple of them are ministers also.Who taught them dishonesty and corruption?"

"No,I don't agree.A man becomes what his environment makes of him.If some one is always living and working in the midst of corruption and is subservient to corrupt people how can he remain honest.No,no.Let him become an honest professor or a researcher."

"Many IAS officers are honest and they have stood steadfast despite political pressure on them putting their career in jeopardy and as a rule it can't be said that all of them succumb to their environment ."

"Ok Baba.Let us agree to disagree.See,unnecessarily we are fighting,why not ask Sanatan himself.Let us see what does he want to become and whatever,he likes we both will help him make that."

"That is nice.I agree."

Sanatan heard all the discussions held between his father and mother and was inclined to go by his mother.When they asked for his choice and future plan,he said that his choice was what his mother liked.It was,at length, decided to arrange for him all facilities along with his further studies to prepare for Civil Services competition.He joined graduation at the university taking political science as the main branch and got an accommodation in a reputed hostel.His mother and father both had come to the city of the university to see him properly settled down and on finding him properly adjusted with the new environ they returned back to their village.

During Dashara vacation Sanatan came back to village to be with his parents for a few days.He found his parents extremely happy to be with him and his mother would cook everything of his liking and ask him so many things about the university,it's academic life and how was he finding the hostel life,whether,meals served to him were tasty or not?

Sanatan gave rosy pictures of some activities and some were of course not to his liking but he was keeping himself centered to his target.however,he was finding one difficulty
that medium of instruction& teaching at the university was English language ,whereas, he had ,so far,been taught in his own language but that he was making up as he knew that general English was a compulsory subject for civil services exams. He continued coming to see his parents whenever there was holiday for a period of over a week.One year passed by and he passed his exams again in flying colors.Second year commenced with a colorful note.Though there were many avenues of distraction but he put all his efforts and energies to maintain his highest standards.Ten months passed off very peacefully with continuance of usual schedule of going to parents and sometimes his father visiting him.His exams were approaching and his concentration was increasing on his target that suddenly one day there was a bolt from the blue.He got the news that his

mother had expired and he was immediately required at home.Without bothering for anything else he rushed to his village with the next available roadways bus.

It was a heartbreaking sight.His mother,the dearest person on the earth who was everything for him,was lying flower bedecked on a bamboo carriage (arthi) and his father had gone hysterical.Some distant relatives,men & women   of the village had gathered and some old persons were busy making all arrangements for the cremation.

He could not bear the agony and fell on the feet of the mortal remains of his mother and started weeping and crying which further disturbed his father.Some people tried to console him but he was totally heart wreck.The mother had passed away about nine hours back and any delay in funeral was not desirable and an elder person of the village suggested his father to control himself and also his son and proceed ahead with further ceremonies.

However,they seemed to be in no mood to heed any attention to what was being advised.A relative came forward and separated away son from the dead body of his mother and shook his father to command the situation and go ahead with funeral proceedings as per religious tenets.Willy nilly they readied for the funeral proceedings and cremation.Next thirteen days both father and son remained engaged with various rituals and ceremonies though being wreck totally.

The exams were very close and it was not proper for Sanatan to remain with father any further.An old teacher from his school who had come to their house to mourn the sad demise advised Sanatan to devote whole heartedly on his studies and march towards fulfilling the desires of his mother and that would be the best homage to the departed soul. Sanatan though still immersed in agony,realized the value of the advice and decided to march ahead taking for granted that his mother was thereafter every moment with him,in his memories,around him and wherever,he may be.He decided to behave like a brave & dedicated soldier of the Indian army and forgetting the loss proceeded ahead in the battlefield of life.

Every moment he remembered his mother,her encouragement to him and her dreams&desires and worked hard which enabled him to get exceptionally high merit in the graduation.During summer vacations he stayed with his father but he found him aloof,cut off,morose and behaving as if he was in some other world.He had lost his interest in everything around him which was causing worry but still he was conscious of him and wanted him to do whatever his mother had desired.That was the only candle flame in the limitless black hole wherein his father had entered and he expected his father to come out of that one day sooner or later.

New academic session was knocking at the doors.He comforted his father in all possible manner and left for the university.He joined post graduation with political science as his subject keeping in target the civil services competitive exams.A couple of months passed by and he felt that by then his father would have regained normalcy but something else was waiting for him in the store of time. One day he received a letter from his father the sight of which delighted him,happily he opened the same and liked to read,

"My dear son,you are the only hope left with me and I would like you to fulfil the ambitions of your mother who would always be watching you from the heavens.I am finding myself here all alone and a deep void has come in me which I want to fill up with some constructive activities away from this environ.I have transferred enough funds to your accounts which would be sufficient to sustain your studies for several years.In addition also I have made arrangement that agriculture & farming continues regularly through some people on sharing basis and they would be depositing half of the earnings to your account.All details I am keeping locked in your mother's box,a key of which is available with you.You are also having a

key of the main door of the house and I would like you to visit sometimes and see that things are moving smoothly at the village.

I exactly don't know of my future plans and the place I shall be putting up but definitely I will be in touch with you at regular intervals,at least a fortnight through my mobile and if possible through letters also.When I am able to forget my agonies and pains and normalcy comes back to me,I will return to our village.I would advise you to remain normal and a fighter as you have been and achieve your desired goal which will give peace to the soul of your mother."

Sanatan fell from sky to the earth.He was not so mature to bear the loss of mother coupled with departure of his father from the arena of active life and that kept him disturbed for several days until he received a call from his father.His father assured him that neither he had relinquished the life nor was going to leave him alone it was rather his effort to forget the things that had been tormenting him and to seek diversion and solace in serving those who were in much greater state of grief,helplessness and nothingness.That dispelled the worries of Sanatan and he plunged himself to work whole heartedly towards his targets.

Days,weeks and months were passing by and Sanatan was concentrating his studies and preparations towards post graduation exams and civil services. Every week or after a lapse of ten day,he would receive a call from his father and discuss about him,his activities and also apprise him of his activities & efforts.A period of six months elapsed that his father informed him during his telecon,

"I am now in an interior area where frequent contact is not possible but you need not worry I will come to some town and keep ringing you periodically.Had I not come to this area I would have never known the realities of life and how life runs with paucity and nothingness.In fact I find these people in so much of pains that I am forgetting my pains.I like to spend

sometimes here to help them in whatever measures I can.You take care of yourself always remembering that those who make dedicated efforts are never losers."

The words of his father were inspiring and invigorating which boosted up his morale and he decided never to look back but work relentlessly to achieve his target.He did wonderfully well in the previous year and maintained same zeal during final year as well.Though concentrating on final year,he was preparing for the civil services preliminaries also.Final year exams were over and and full efforts were then for the competitive examinations.He knew that there were only three chances available between the age of twenty one years to twenty four years for competing in the civi services and any failure at any step could be very costly.

He left nothing to chance and with all round full preparations faced different examinations and got selected in the Indian Administrative Service in the very first attempt itself. During his next tele conversation with his father he apprised him of his success. Father was very pleased & happy and had long discussion with him. Sanatan did notice that his father though expressed to be very happy but he was hiding something and some deep pain,apprehension or agony was lying clandestine behind his voice as he said,

"life is an endless canvas of pains and on this canvas nature paints here & there some happy moments for each one of us and let those be our beacon lights under the guidance of which let life be directed towards our defined goals.
My son, to-morrow I may not be there with you but I wish you to achieve what you look for."

Sanatan remembered happy moments spent with his mother and remembered her desires & wishes only forgetting every thing else.He wound up himself,left the university,he left the hostel and came back to his home to re-live those happy moments when her mother's lap was available to him,her love& affection was flowing endlessly for him and her encouragements,motivation and blessings were showing him the path even in darkness.

Being relaxed in solitude for some days,he joined Indian Administrative Service at Lal Bahadur Shastri National Academy in Mussorie. He continuously worked hard and his performance made him a recognized budding officer,however,something happened to him one night which he never revealed to any one that he suddenly left the Academy and went away somewhere leaving behind his colleagues,friends,teachers and the director of the Academy surprised.People expected that he may come back after some days but that did not happen.

CHAPTER.VI-The Swings .

Roshani was doing fairly well in her graduation classes and had settled down at the post graduate degree college.She was residing at the college hostel and had been granted a backward community scholarship by the state government. Sanatan had also made arrangement that every month she was getting a fixed amount of money.The total amount was sufficient for her expenses.Every week she would get a ring from Sanatan who would encourage her to concentrate on her studies and in turn she would remind him to complete his task and come back to her soon.During holidays and vacations she would come to her village to be with her parents.Her progress in life had created a sense of satisfaction to her parents which had resulted in improvement of her father's health.He was by then much improved and was able to move & take care of his normal village activities.

"I have got something which is asking me to be here on one hand and on the other hand I can't think of a life beyond you.I am in a fix what to do but one thing I am very clear that I will have to find out what I am searching for.No doubt I have identified the source, the person who can get me information but I don't know why he is tight lipped."Said Sanatan during his call to Roshani.

"Give him some time.May be he is assessing you before he decides to come out."Suggested Roshani.

"That is what I have guessed.I am giving him time to win my confidence and also have faith in me."

"Otherwise how is he?"

"He is a wonderful person,well versed with everything of the area and he has taken service to needy people as his mission and is always helping me."

"Then why don't you indoctrinate him to take up whole heartedly the quest and mission which you have and you come here and take command of the things at this place."

"You are right.That is my ultimate planning but let me find out what has happened to my father and where exactly he is and whether he is alive or dead? Once I find that answer my search here would be over."

" Ok.Better you search all possible sources and find out the answer."

"Thanks .But till then you have to wait."

They had long discussion on several topics covering personal & family matters and their own thoughts and course of future life.

Normally Roshani used to feel very relaxed and encouraged after having talks with Sanatan but that day something was pinching her but she was not able to locate that and was feeling restless and disturbed.That night when she retired to bed,she could not sleep and remained immersed in thoughts and memories as if many chapters of past were unfolding themselves before her eyes as video clips.

"Baba,excuse me;how many members are there in your family?"

"Why do you want to know that?"
"I am trying to see how best I can help you."

She remembered to have seen an young man clad in clean but ordinary clothes,having a cloth bag hanging on his left shoulder and wearing a chappal in name of footwear,had come to her house quite late in the morning. He said namaste to her father and requested him to help him answer his questions.

"There are three members in my family,myself,my wife and my daughter."
"Thanks.If you don't mind ,could I meet them."
There was some element of hesitation in the mind of Baba,he paused and pondered over for a few minutes and then said,
"Ok. I call them.You meet them."

He called for his wife and daughter to come out of house to see the gentleman who wanted to meet them.

"She is my wife." He pointed towards an elderly lady.

*"She is my daughter."*He pointed towards a girl who might be around ten years of age.

Sanatan wished them both with folded hands and introduced himself to them,

"I am Sanatan, a volunteer of the Charity Organization.I am staying in the next village in a room in the school premises.My mission is to help develop people in these villages,educate them on health & hygiene,remove superstition and other evils prevailing in the society and encourage child education and whatever other problems I come to notice or people need my help."

"Oh,good.We have heard some thing about the volunteers.To-day we are seeing you as the first volunteer who has come to our house."

"I will be frequently visiting and taking care in whatever manner I can do."

"Good ,any thing else."

"Gradually you will know me better and I will know you all.But please let me know ,whether, your daughter is studying."

Again there was an element of hesitation. Husband and wife both started starring at each other without a reply,at that point daughter herself intervened and spoke,

"I am Roshani,I have studied up to third standard beyond that my studies could not continue.I am helping my mother and father in house hold activities."
"But why.School is available up to matriculation in the village where I am staying and that is next to your village."

Again there was a pause and hesitation. Her mother replied,
"See,we are very poor people,we cannot afford and also our society does not permit girls reading much.When we get a proper groom we marry the daughter and she goes away to her groom's house."
"That is not good.I will convince you and one day I am sure you will send your daughter for further studies."

Sanatan discussed several social & personal problems and then went away to some other houses of the village. Roshani,on that day got an idea that she could study further but how?Though still she was not sure that she would be able to go ahead with her studies hanging on the altar of many ifs and buts but still an spark had been kindled in her and she had to wait & see if that could ignite a flame.

After a week Sanatan reappeared at her house. Roshani greeted him and took him to her parents. He stayed there for half an hour,discussed several issues and further education to their daughter but their reply remained negative.This process of coming of Sanatan and his efforts of convincing her parents continued,however,without any positive outcome.After a couple of months,Sanatan narrated to them a true story which had happened some days back in a village where also Sanatan was going for his work. He narrated the story,

"There is a family like you in the village Nagala about fifteen kilometers away from here. A fortnight back the head of family has suddenly died due to some accident.He was also having a daughter like you.They are not having any means of livelihood and the daughter is quite grown up;the mother and daughter both are in trouble.Had daughter been educated,she would have been of support to her mother.God,forbid if something happens to any one of you,then what is going to happen; can you guess?"

That episode hit the bull's eye and they agreed to consider educating their daughter further but there was again some hitch,

"The matriculation school is in the village where you are staying,that is not very near and now Roshani is a fairly grown up girl,her safety in commuting to and fro and then girl's toilet etc.would be a problem."
Expressed her father.
"Don't worry girl's toilet is available in that school and I am trying some more girls

from this village,that will solve your problem of commuting to and fro.If worst comes and I fail to get some more girls from this village,I will make some alternate arrangement."Replied Sanatan.

"Ok.Agreed. But she will be much elder to the boys and girls in her class and for several years her studies have got discontinued.She will find difficulties to cope up with the course and it's understanding."

"Worry not.I am myself going to conduct coaching classes on every Sunday for the whole day and would make up for the loss of studies for all such girls.And let us not think of her age,it is hardly a matter of two three years."

After a week Sanatan again came and told her parents that three more girls from that village were ready for admission in that school and they were practically of the same age but still in lower classes.They wanted to study but their parents had not permitted mainly because of toilet problem.He further assured to see that no inconvenience was caused to any of the girls.That proved as the harbinger of change in the life of Roshani.

Roshani had passed ninth standard and was going to join last step of the matriculation.She was at the last leg of puberty and many physical and emotional changes had been taking place in her.She was no more the same girl who would concentrate on the work which was assigned to her and also be routinely following the house hold activities the way mother wanted.She was feeling something in her body and mind.She used to consider Sanatan as her mentor and guide who was there to help her,her family members and also help them whenever,they had any sort of problem.She had been developing a very unique feeling towards Sanatan.While she was liking to spend more & more time with Sanatan,she was also feeling an attachment to him and would like to share each and everything with him.The intensity of that feeling went on increasing day by day and by the time she completed her tenth standard she had the very clear idea that her feeling was love for Sanatan but question was how to verify that and express same to him and how would he respond and react as he had always looked cool and detached person.It was becoming difficult for her to contain her feelings and flood of emotions. She at length expressed that to her mother,

"Mother,Sanatan has been doing so much for us for the last so many years and he has never expected anything from us,should we not do something for him."
"What do you want to do?"
"We may offer him food and sweets during festivals."
"I guess you have something else in your mind."
"What else?No,no nothing."
"See,I can guess,probably you like him or love him."
"He looks to be a very cool man,I don't know,what will he think about me."
"If you have something tell me.I will talk."
"Some day you just whisper and see."
"MyGod! So much you are keeping concealed.Ok ,I will see."

Roshani   had cleared the last leg of the matriculation from the same school.   The fire in her gut,the intensity of flame burning i n   h e r   m i n d   w a s   c o n t i n u o u s l y increasing,possibly that was the demand of a female adolescent entering the doors of adulthood.Her father was feeling weak for sometimes and   finding himself difficult to move.One day he had developed severe pains in his back which Sanatan noticed during his routine visit to their house and offered him some medicines.her mother requested him to stay that night with them and have meals whatever,they could normally afford.With a lot of hesitation he accepted the request on the condition that he would take the simplest possible meals the way they took daily.

After dinner Sanatan wanted to go out for some walk   but Roshani's mother advised him not to venture in the darkness as it was not safe in that area due to wild cats rather she liked to have some chit chat before they retired to bed.

"You have done a lot for us,you have practically changed our life,what inspires you for that?" Asked Roshani's mother.

"I seek pleasure in helping others who are weak and deprived and also keep myself busy to forget my own agonies and pains."Replied Sanatan.

"What are the pains that you have and can we do something?"

"No.My pains and problems are absolutely mine.Something is lotted to me and something is my own creation."

"But still sharing may lessen your burden and possibly lighten you."

"I know but I don't like to burden some body with my pains."

"Have faith,we will be happy to be of some help to you."

"Ok.But not to-day.I may have to load myself with those memories and to-day I am lighter and don't like to go in memory lanes."

"Do you love some one who may share with you."

"My most loved one is my mother who is in heavens and I don't know the whereabouts

of my father who was my protector and guide."

She observed that Sanatan had become morose and tears had started rolling down over his cheeks and he was not able to continue discussions further.She tried to comfort him and changed the direction of their talks but not to avail.She remained with him for sometimes and then asked him to relax and sleep over the cot and leaving him there went inside the house. Roshani was busy in the kitchen cleaning up the utensils and   winding up every thing there.In a slow but sweet voice mother spoke to daughter,

"I find something very pinching in the life of Sanatan which he does not like to open out but that is haunting him. If somehow he gets confidence in some one then he may open out and something could be done."
"I also have felt something like that but he avoids talking on his personal issues."
"I see a shine in his eyes when he meets you,why not you develop close ness and see if he responds.After all he is also

young and some change is easily possible in him."
"I will try."

Roshani said to her mother that in fact she wanted that and then things were clear for her to try her own methods to develop close ness to him.the most difficult problem before Roshani was to assess the reaction of Sanatan if she advanced to give inkling of her feelings.She decided to keep herself near him for more & more of time and talk to him on personal front.One day when he seemed to be in a little happier mood,she invited him to go on next Sunday to nearby hillock to watch the reddening beauty of setting sun and the vast expanse of villages around that and how serene & beautiful they appeared in the dusk when the mushrooming clouds of smoke emanated from the houses from burning of wood and dried cow dung.They went to the top or the hillock and sat there side by side.Still there was some time for sun to set but it had got ready to dive in the ocean of western horizon. Roshani suddenly asked,

"Would you like to talk if I ask you something."
"Why not.Why do you doubt,I always speak to you all."
"How do I look to you?"

He paused for some moments,looked to her from top to toe and then replied,

"Very nice.In fact wonderful,an unique person."
"Do you like me?"
"My God ! You have brought me here to ask such a question.You should have yourself read me from my eyes and behavior.I understand women are very keen observers of male psychology."
"I find certain anomalies in your behavior,you behave much older than your age.It becomes difficult to assess what is really going on in your mind & heart."

"You are partly right but something is there in you which attracts me towards you but my mind asks me to be aloof ."
"Whenever,there is a conflict between heart and mind,better go by heart,that will always tell you the truth,the inner truth and also that will never betray you."
"Oh,my God! You are so clear in your thoughts.I will remember your words."
"So accept and without hesitation express what your heart says.An opportunity

missed may be missed for ever and may never come back.When the time is gone only repentance remains."
"So my young teacher,whatever,you advise I accept.I definitely like you."
"Thank God! My good fortune."

That gentle outburst of feelings and their expression made both of them lighter and delighted.They enjoyed the divine beauty of setting sun and the smoky dusk and returned back. Roshani liked him to stay with them that night but he thankfully declined as he had recently got a jeep from his sponsors for the good work he was doing over a large number of villages of that area and next morning he had planned to go to a remote village.

Roshani told her mother that Sanatan also had a liking for her which added fuel to the fire and thereafter she got a freedom to mingle with him within the unwritten frame work of customs & traditions prevailing in their society.Time was flying away on its wings and Roshani and Sanatan both were concentrating on their respective activities,however,also giving a subtle & serene growth to their love.

She had joined higher secondary classes at a college located in a nearby small town. He had arranged a bicycle for her to commute to and fro and many times when the weather was inclement he would take her to college by his jeep and also help her come back home.She was doing fairly good in her studies and had crossed eleventh standard with flying colors and had gone to the twelfth standard maintaining her diligent efforts.

The month of January was coming to an end,the exams of Roshani were getting on the anvil and visit of Sanatan had lessened to their village as he was concentrating more on some new area.One day he heard through someone that her father was in bad shape and was neither able to stand up properly nor walk.He came to see him next day and examined his problems and physical condition.He administered him some medications for osteoporosis and advised him to use a strong cloth bandage around his waist and also to consult experts who were likely to visit on behalf of another non-government organization at a camp to be organized in a nearby location.On that day Roshani's mother took him inside the house under the pretext of offering some eatables and straight away asked him,

"Do you like Roshani."
"Yes."
"Do you love her."
"Yes."
"If she decides to marry you,how would you respond?"
"Let her decide that first."

The last episode that flashed before the mind of Roshani was that of a fortnight before he expressed to move on some new assignment for a couple of years.Roshani had finished her exams and one afternoon she had taken him to the same spot wherefrom once they had enjoyed the sunset and the smoky dusk.She was talking about his personal life and relations,

"You know each and every thing about me and my parents,but you never told us anything about yourself. Can you tell us something?"

"It gives me pains to go back into the memory lanes but any way you must know something.I belong to a fairly decent & prosperous family wherefrom still I get regular earnings.I had joined the highest cadre of this country but that also I left.I loved my mother most but she has become a star in the sky and I don't know where my father has disappeared searching for the soul of my mother.And I am searching for both of them through happiness in others."

"I appreciate your feelings and efforts.Had you not come here I would have never grown literate and would have continued to be a wild creature.But I have seen only nothingness,paucity and poverty and a spark has got kindled in me to have a reasonable life devoted to goodness."

"Then better you join me."

"I have to join you but not as a volunteer of any organization.I like to have a peaceful settled life with you and spread education

through teaching in a school of our own.This country is still in the darkness of illiteracy,superstition and poverty and I want to light small small lamps the glow of which can help improve the situation in huts & hutments of poor and helpless people."

"Ok.Agreed.But not here,you will have to come to my village and live in my parental house and behave as a person of that area."

"Accepted."

Since then Roshani had started thinking & dreaming of a life which was a normal family life coupled with service to poor & deprived children as she herself was,to teach them,to educate them,to uplift them and to make them good human beings.She also used to dream that once she was well settled she would take her parents with her or help them to have a decent life in her parental village itself.

The memories of the bygone days were the biggest asset of Roshani and she was concentrating herself on her studies.The regular periodical calls from Sanatan were continuously encouraging her.There was a normalcy running in the life which saw her having crossed the first year of graduation.When she was over half way in the graduation final year the periodicity of telephone calls became erratic and they became few and far between which were worrying her and on enquiries Sanatan would say that he was extremely engaged in the work left half way by his father and was trying to complete them in a time bound manner and he was receiving great help from the person who had been the right hand of his father,Biru Mahato but still who had not disclosed him the truth of his father's disappearance.

It was the last day of her final year exam,she had done very well in that last paper and had come back in a delightful mood. She was so happy that she herself wanted to ring Sanatan that evening and share her happiness with him.In the afternoon when she was relaxing in her hostel room she received a registered letter which as per sender's address was from

Sanatan. She was surprised to see such a letter and was thoughtful as to why such a step had been taken by him without telling her.But feeling that there could be some surprise gift she opened the envelope.She was really surprised to find a set of documents annexed with a letter from Sanatan. Those documents were stamped &issued by a court of law.The letter was purely personal having long content written in own hand writing but the last but one para was very small and read,

"I have willed in your name all my parental properties in my village and all my assets and liabilities including all the bank accounts maintained in my name.I am longing for a dream of having a happy conjugal life with you serving humanity in the way you wanted.I am trying my best to complete the jobs which my father could not finish but I have some premonitions,I don't know why.God,forbid if some thing happens to me I wish you to take command of the situation with courage & mettle and live your life happily the way you have dreamt of to live."

All the happiness that Roshani had,suddenly disappeared and she found herself in the wilderness of worries and emotions but still keeping herself cool she decided to ring him in the evening and scold him for making such a nasty will.But alas! in the evening she went on ringing and ringing,however,there was no response from the other end.

Chapter VII.The Truth.

Several months had elapsed but the contact from Sanatan was missing ,neither a ring had come from him nor there was any response,whenever,she tried to contact him.It had perplexed her and her parents and they were getting laden with many wild imaginations about his well being and of course his intentions as well.Though Roshani had passed her graduation with a first class and had desire to go ahead with higher studies but she was in a dilemma and did not opt for continuance of her studies unless and until she was able to know of her consort-in-waiting.She had thought of contacting Biru Mahato but she could not get any contact details of him.As a matter of chance she could locate the envelope which had come to her as the registered letter from him carrying his will and aroused in her a hope to write to him and to know what exactly was happening causing breakdown in communication from him.She immediately wrote a detailed letter to him and posted the same via registered post.A fortnight passed but no reply was received. Her worries and anxieties went up by leaps & bounds.Another week passed and one day she received back her own envelope undelivered.That enveloped her and her parents under the cloud of something unfortunate which might have happened to Sanatan.She was left only with one option and that was to go to the place wherefrom registered letter had come and find the whereabouts of Sanatan.

Roshani set out herself on a long and unknown voyage in search of truth which had kept her bewildered for several months and which was the milestone of her future and life.She travelled for several hours in a train which brought her to a station where from she had to travel by bus route to reach the place where Sanatan was residing.The train journey and the bus journey both had been something quite new for her and the route and the place were totally unknown to her but she was continuing on her journey only in the hope that she may be able to recover and meet her love-the love which was away from her for some years & months.While traveling in the bus ,she noticed a crossroad,a square in the centre of which a bust was erected and the face of the bust was resembling with the face of Sanatan.She was shocked,she was surprised,she was astonished to see that bust as the flash of idea came to his mind that how come Sanatan's bust was there.Bus took a right turn from that square and she noticed a board reading as Sadanand Marg(Sadanand Road). She was doubly shocked.Though she could not exactly recollect the name Sadanand,but she continuously felt that name to have heard earlier and somehow that seemed to be familiar.Under the dual shock of two names she travelled for half an hour and she reached the place of her destination.

She enquired some gentleman about a reasonable place of stay who advised her a small hotel where she went by a cycle rickshaw and took a room for a week's time.She relaxed for some times,took bath,got herself readied up,took snacks in the hotel restaurant and enquired them about the locality where she was to go in search of Sanatan. She came to the house as per the address and found the same locked. With the help of nearby people she located the land lord and went to his house to enquire about Sanatan.

"I understand Sanatana has been your tenant."
"Yes,He is my tenant but who are you?"
"I am his fiancée.We have lost contact with him for several months and also my registered letter sent to him has come back undelivered.I have come here to find him out."
"He has been a perfect gentleman and paying my rent very regularly but for over six months neither he has met me nor sent my rent.On some occasions I went to find him out but his room was locked.I also don't know ,where is he."
"Can you tell me some body who can help me?"
"I have seen only one man who always used to be with him.His name is Biru Mahato. I will give you his address."

She had fallen from sky to palm tree. She was well versed with the name and activities of Biru Mahato but again she had to locate him.Next day very early morning she got herself ready,she took a quick breakfast and some packed lunch and set out herself in search of Biru Mahato. She had hired a jeep and using that wandered from place to place. Wherever,she went people told her to know of Biru and Sanatan and they also told to have not seen Sanatan for quite a long time but where was he only Biru could tell.Evenjng was approaching and she was losing her hope that Biru could be located in a village busy in helping people.She met him and introduced herself to him.Biru was extremely happy to meet her and greeted her with open heart and enthusiasm but suddenly his happiness disappeared and he became morose.She enquired about Sanatan to which he was hesitant and only said,

"To-day if you like you can stay with me or I leave you to the place of your stay and be at rest.To morrow I want to show you

something and tell you in details everything.I know you can not tolerate any delay but pardon me I will have to show you and tell you many things."

He came with Roshani to the hotel,dropped her there and went back.

Next morning Biru came to the hotel and took Roshani with him.They went to the room where Sanatan stayed.Biru had a duplicate key of the lock and using the same he opened the lock.They went inside the room.everything inside the room was lying well placed but covered with a thick layer of the dust indicating that they had not been wiped clean for many days.There were two cupboards in the room.Sanatan opened them one by one.There was a very beautiful bridal attire hanging on a hanger and a large number of other ladies ornaments and crafts were lying kept therein.The other Cupboard had clothing and personal items of Sanatan and several letters and other documents. Biru showed her ladies items and explained,

" Bhai(brother) was in a great hurry. He wanted to complete his work and go back to you .He had purchased all these items for you.These are the pieces of beauty & elegance made by artisans and craftsmen of this area.The bridal dress was specially ordered by him. He wanted you to wear this at the time of wedding.He used to say that he would fix the dates,go to your place and marry you without delay.He wanted me also to accompany him and help arrange everything for his marriage."
"But where is he,why don't you tell me."
"I will have to tell you and will definitely tell you."

The behavior of Biru had given enough inkling to Roshani that something was not alright but still she wanted to listen from horse's mouth.She was full of tears and as she was looking at each item she was drowning deep into thoughts of those moments which were hers and also those which may not be hers and every piece kept for her were adding to her tears and flood of emotions.Biru could guess that and advised her to go to some other place.He took her to a village where he used to go to serve an ailing family.

She met the elders who were in eighties. They had all praise for him but were in tears as he had not visited them for several months. He was not only attending on them but also helping them in many ways including financial help. Biru took her to Several other houses and everywhere she got the same expression of feelings.

Biru requested her to accompany him to some other place. They both travelled for about an hour and reached to the road to which she had read as Sadanand Marg.Biru took her to a spot where there was still a deep ditch on the road and fragments and pieces of a broken vehicle were seen lying scattered on the road sides.

"Why have you brought me here and what do you want to show me?" Roshani asked him angrily.
"This is the place which has become pilgrimage for me and all those people

whom Bhai ji was serving and until a memorial is made here,we will not allow any body to disturb any thing from this place." He replied.
"Memorial ! What for?"
"For the sacrifice,for the martyrdom of Bhai ji."
"What do you mean?"
"Whatever, I said. For us he is a martyr."
"You explain to me in details what all you know and can tell me."
"Evening is approaching,let us go back.I know to-night will be very heavy & never ending for you but Bhai ji always told me about you to be strong-Will person. To-morrow I will answer every thing whatsoever you want."

Things had become very clear and beyond doubt that Sanatan was no more.It was the greatest shock of her life and she had found herself in the black hole of the universe with nothing around her. That night had become Himalayan to her and colder than Siachen glacier.

The sun rose with the new dawn and Roshani got up as usual but without vital force in her veins & nerves. She followed her morning routine as a robot and readied herself,however, feeling devoid of life and enveloped in the anxieties of future uncertainties.Around ten o'clock there was a knock at her door and the waiter informed her of Biru waiting for her in the lounge.She came down and met him as an extinguished lamp though she was still eager to know answer to various questions.Seeing her Biru stood up from his chair and paid his respect.She sat before him in the chair. Biru was not surprised with this but was worried to bring her back to life for the jobs ahead.

"I understand your mental condition but time cycle can not be put on back gear and life has to go on and you have to gather courage to face the things," Said Biru.
"I know but where is the point of life for me." Replied Roshani.
"See,I have experienced such a situation thrice,when my parents were killed,when Sada Babu was murdered and then when

Bhai ji met with tragic death and I had no reason to continue in normal life but every time something happened which brought me back to life.However,you are having at least memories of Bhai ji and responsibilities of your parents."

"You are right. You are elder to me ,please advise me what should I do?"

" Good,treat me as your elder brother and do as I tell."

"Ok !what should I do?"

"Be ready.We will go to Sanatan's house,collect separately all his personal dresses and belongings and all other items which he had purchased and collected for you,his books and letters etc.There is a goddess temple which is the prime deity of this area and where Bhai ji used to go very often. Let us go there with all his personal belongings.There you worship the deity and distribute all his belongings to poor people,beggars and urchins. The other set will be for you,which you carry with you."

They went to the Sanatan's residence and collected all his clothes and other belongings and went to the temple which was four kilometers away. She worshipped the mother goddess invoking her blessings to show the right path and distributed all items to poors.The temple environment was calm,peaceful,serene and subtle where Roshani liked to sit for sometimes beneath a banyan tree. While sitting there she felt mother goddess standing in front of her,touching her forehead gently and advising her to stand calm and composed and then she blessed her for a good future and disappeared. That touch gave her invisible strength and she called Biru near her and wanted to know the details of various events.

"You mentioned that Bhaiji's father was murdered,what exactly had happened"
"Though I never told Bahiji of this truth but he had come to know of it.In fact his father Sadanad Sarkar popularly known as Sadaa Babu was like father to me and he had given me a new life and meaning of life after my parents had been killed by Naxalites.
He was a great crusader & reformer and I was always with him.He had eradicated

many social evils prevalent here and was educating people.Some traders involved in human trafficking and looting jungle wealth were finding him as obstacle.Sadaa Babu had received several threatening letters and calls also but he was not worried.Once he told me about BhaiJi having become a very big officer.There after he had become careless. One evening he insisted me to remain at my home and he was going to his residence all alone that some henchmen of those unscrupulous traders brutally killed him.Though police people could find out the culprits but the case was hushed up."

"Oh! So sad, probably that's why your BhaiJi insisted to come here possibly to know the truth.Did you notice anything peculiar in your Bahiji?"

"Nothing.He was a very good and helpful person.When he became very close to me,he used to mention about you and the promise that he had made to you.-----------------------"

There was a pause for a few moments as if he was trying to recollect something then he added,

One late Sunday evening I had come to his residence for knowing next day's program,I went on knocking & knocking at the door but he did not respond then I pushed the doors. It got opened,I saw him sitting behind a burning candle and concentrating on the flame.Probably he was seeing something."

"Oh! That is a science which he knew but was rarely using.Something did he tell you?"

" One day he told me that I would have to take responsibility to continue the work which his father was doing and he had also followed."

"Did he tell you any reason."

"He only said,that was the scene of future."

"Did he know of his death?"

"May be,but definitely he was in a great hurry to go back to you.One morning suddenly he called me and asked me to accompany him to the court and get an advocate.He wanted to get some legal document prepared."

"What did you do?"

"We,went to the court and located an advocate.He got something made on a stamp paper and same was submitted to the magistrate.The magisterial action was complete by the evening but he could not receive back the papers.Next day he asked me to go to a particular village and he himself would go to the court,collect the papers,post them and join me by afternoon in that village."

"Did he join back?"

"No.He did not come to that village.In the evening we came to know that there was some mine blast on the road and in that a jeep had blown off.We rushed to the spot and found police there searching for the clues.I identified that as Bhaiji's jeep.Police collected pieces of bones and flesh and assembled them as the mortal remains of BhaiJi. After completing all legal formalities police handed me over his mortal remains.As the news spread people from different villages assembled and they wanted his cremation with full state honor which the civil authorities agreed and accordingly everything was arranged."

"Oh,my God! Such an end to such a good man.What is happening in this country how will somebody remain a noble person?"

"I am also unfortunate to see horrible death of all those who were near and dear to me,but I will have to do,what BhaiJi has desired."

"Did Naxalites kill him?"

"No.They had planted land mine on the road as they had information that convoy of a big political personality was to pass that way but to our misfortune BhaiJi passed that way.Naxalites also regretted but we took it very seriously."

"How were the funeral rites done."

"All the people wherever, he used to visit had contributed for expenses and I had worked as the main person.Everything had been done with full religious rites and as per our customs & traditions.On the last day of rites all people gathered,had taken a pledge to fight against Naxalites and all those who indulged in disruptive activities."

"You knew about me,why did you not inform me."

"I tried my best but I could not get your contact details.Bhaiji's mobile had also

gone off in the blast.I had no option but to pray God,that some day I may meet you."
"While coming to this place my bus had passed through a square where I saw a bust resembling to that of Sanatan's face and a road named as SadanandMarg.What is that?"
After his death all village people & local leaders had pressed civil authorities for erecting his bust and naming a road in his father's name. It was done to meet our demand.That square is now known as Sanatan Chowk.But still our demand for erecting a memorial at the place of his death stands."

Roshani had got all that she could get and decided to return back.All the items which were meant for her were collected,packed and taken to her hotel room.Along with Biru she went to the house of land lord and liked to pay him the rent for the period it had not been paid.He had a great respect & regard for Sanatan and he declined to accept anything from her.She asked him,why did he not tell her of his death when she met him for the first time to which he replied that he had no courage to do so.

During the night in her hotel room,She was going through various letters and other documents collected from the residence of Sanatan.A note written on his last night before his death,meant for her was quite long and touching.As she was reading the lines and words she was not able to control & contain herself but she found a small para reading as,

"I have seen my fate and future a couple of days back & the time is running out of my hands.I want to reach you without delay but I don't want to take chance.I have willed everything that is mine to you.Despite having opportunity,I could not fulfill the ambition of my mother and chose the path of my father.I have realized that I should have continued at your place.In case I am not able to meet you,I will be leaving behind all my assets,liabilities and responsibilities to you."

EPILOGUE.

Roshani had lost all her dreams that she had been nurturing for so many years and the person who had moulded & reshaped her destiny had become the lost dream of her destiny.There was no meaning of her staying any more at the place and she decided to leave that place very next day itself.It were the memories,the documents& papers and various items&garments collected from his residence which were going to be with her as the relics of her love.Next morning she called for Biru Mahato and expressed her desire to return back.He advised her to stay for a day or two more to arrange for railway reservation since as such a long journey in the train without that would be very troublesome and that he also wanted to arrange a homage to the departed soul by all the villagers in her presence but she was not ready to relent,however,she assured him to be definitely present during the inauguration of their proposed memorial.

Biru insisted that as an elder brother it was his bounden duty to see that she reached back her place safely and therefore he also wanted to travel with her,which at length she agreed. Biru liked a time period of two hours to pack up for his journey and in the meantime she would also pack up and be ready to move.She called for the jeep that she had been hiring,cleared the hotel bills and finally bade good bye to the place where she had come in search of her love and had lost it.

She and Biru both set out on the journey.She liked to go to the spot of blast where her love had become a heap of flesh and bones.She asked him to stand a little away from her.She took a round of the ditch caused due to blast and bent herself to the ground.She took a pinch of dust from the soil and put that on her forehead as vermilion applied by married Hindu ladies.Suddenly she felt a wave of some celestial energy in her body and mind with gloom having vanished.She took another pinch of dust in her right hand palm and spoke,

"Lord Sun,Mother Earth and all creatures ,animate & inanimate here and around be the witness.I swear to fulfill the desire of Sanatan's mother and will come back to this place as an Indian Administrative Service(IAS) officer and will see that anything left undone is taken care of.May God! almighty and the soul of my lost love be with me always & ever."

Biru was carefully observing her and listening to what all she spoke.His respect & regard for her went up sky high.She came back to the jeep and both of them marched ahead to the railway station.As she approached the Sanatan Chowk,she asked the jeep driver to halt and park the same at a safe place.She asked Biru to purchase a flower garland taking which she went to the Sanatan's bust.She climbed over the pedestal and put the garland in the neck of the bust.She came down stood before the bust with folded hands,paid her tearful tributes and said,
"I would have never allowed you to come here,had I known that you will never meet me again."

About the Book

"Will You Ever Meet Me Again,"is a saga of love,sacrifice and commitment.

An young man of a prosperous family who had a bright future in hand could not withstand the loss of his parents and left everything and set out himself in search of happiness through service to others,met with an young girl of an unprivileged family.While making all possible efforts to uplift the downtrodden people both fell in love,a chaste love,with each other.

The young man had opportunity to fulfil the ambitions of his late mother but preferred to go on the path of service to poor as adopted by his father and ultimately became the victim of disruptive elements.

His consort in waiting treated herself as his wife and committed to fulfil the ambitions of his mother.

About the Author

A doctorate in chemistry from the University of Allahabad in India Author has spent his life with high energy materials in government of India. After being free from the government service,he is devoting his time & energy for the cause of alleviating sufferings and his writings are inspired from such efforts.

About a dozen of books written in English and Hindi have come out through create space self publishing.

Will You Ever Meet Me Again